D1275534

First
Facts

Our Government

The U.S.
Presidency

by Muriel L. Dubois

Consultant:
Steven S. Smith
Kate M. Gregg Professor of Social Sciences
Washington University, St. Louis, Missouri

Capstone
press
Mankato, Minnesota

First Facts is published by Capstone Press
151 Good Counsel Drive, P.O. Box 669, Mankato, Minnesota 56002
http://www.capstone-press.com

Library of Congress Cataloging-in-Publication Data
Dubois, Muriel L.
   The U.S. presidency/ by Muriel L. Dubois.
   p. cm.—(First facts: Our government)
   Summary: Introduces the executive branch of the United States government
and the role of the president.
   Includes bibliographical references and index.
   ISBN 0-7368-2289-5 (hardcover)
   1. Presidents—United States—Juvenile literature. [1. Presidents.
2. United States—Politics and government.] I. Title. II. Series.
JK517.D83 2004
352.23′0973—dc21   2002155446

Editorial Credits

Christine Peterson, editor; Jennifer Schonborn, series and book designer; Jo Miller, photo
   researcher; Eric Kudalis, product planning editor

Photo Credits

AP/Wide World Photos/J. Scott Applewhite, 9
Corbis, 20; Bettmann, 5
Folio Inc., 19; Everett C. Johnson, cover
Getty Images/Hulton Archive, 11; David Friedman, 13
PhotoDisc Inc., 15
Photri-Microstock, 7, 16, 17

1 2 3 4 5 6 08 07 06 05 04 03

Table of Contents

The President Is a Leader

The president of the United States leads the country. President Franklin D. Roosevelt was a strong leader in hard times. In the 1930s, millions of people did not have jobs. Roosevelt came up with new laws to help people. His leadership helped the country get through the hard times.

 Fun Fact:

President Roosevelt (seated first from right) started the Civilian Conservation Corps (CCC) in 1933. More than 3 million men worked for the CCC.

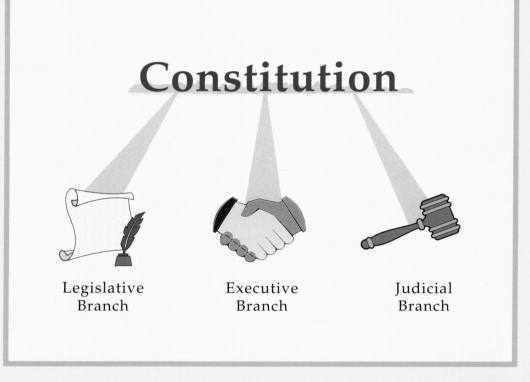

Constitution

Legislative
Branch

Executive
Branch

Judicial
Branch

The U.S. government has three parts. The
legislative branch writes and passes new laws.
The judicial branch explains the laws.

The president is in charge of the executive branch. This branch of the U.S. government makes sure laws are being followed.

The President's Job

The president is the leader of the country. Presidents sign bills into laws. They also suggest new bills to Congress. Presidents make agreements with other countries. They are in charge of the military. They also help choose judges and other government officials.

 Fun Fact:
Presidents use special pens to sign bills. They give the pens to people who helped pass the bill.

9

Who Can Be President?

Candidates for president must meet certain requirements. They must be at least 35 years old when they take office. They must be born in the United States or born to U.S. citizens. Presidents must have lived in the United States for at least 14 years.

Four former U.S. presidents are, from left, Jimmy Carter, George H.W. Bush, William J. Clinton, and Gerald Ford.

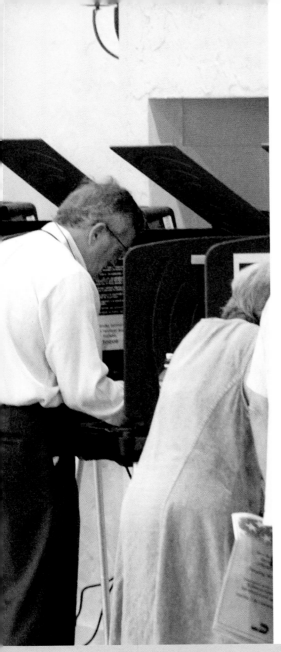

How We Elect a President

Americans vote for a president every four years. Citizens must be 18 years old to vote. A president serves a term that lasts four years. A president can be elected to serve only two terms for a total of eight years.

 Fun Fact:
In 1789, leaders from each state elected the first president, George Washington.

The President's House

The White House is the president's home and office. Presidents and their families live in the White House. Presidents and their staff work in the West Wing of the White House. The president works in the Oval Office.

 Fun Fact:

President John Quincy Adams owned a pet alligator that he kept in the White House.

Presidents work long days. They read notes and make phone calls in the Oval Office. Presidents hold meetings with their staff.

Presidents give speeches and go to
important events. They meet with
members of Congress. Presidents meet
with leaders from other countries.

The President's Cabinet

Presidents choose people to help them. They are part of the president's cabinet. Fifteen men and women make up the cabinet. These members lead important government offices. They give presidents advice about running the country.

 Fun Fact:
Cabinet members sit around an oval table. Presidents always sit in the middle on the table's east side.

Amazing But True!

President Abraham Lincoln's famous beard was the idea of a young girl. In a letter, 11-year-old Grace Bedell told Lincoln he would look better with a beard. Lincoln liked Grace's idea, and he grew a beard. Lincoln kept his beard for the rest of his life.

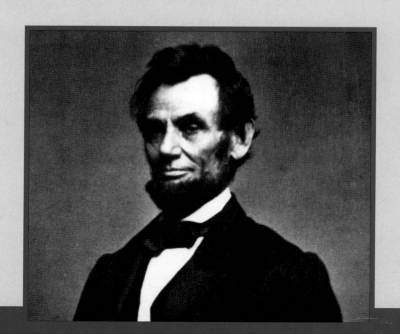

Hands On: Write the President

What would you like the president to do for the country? Tell the president in a letter. Follow these steps to write a letter to the president.

What You Need

Paper   Envelope
Pencil   Postage Stamp

What You Do

1. Begin the letter with the greeting "Dear Mr. President."
2. Write down your ideas for the president. Tell the president about your family, school, or city.
3. Use "thank you" or "sincerely" to end your letter.
4. Sign the letter with your name, age, and address.
5. Place the letter in an envelope.
6. Put a postage stamp on the top right corner of the envelope.
7. Mail the letter to: The President
                            The White House
                            1600 Pennsylvania Avenue NW
                            Washington, DC   20500

Glossary

branch (BRANCH)—a part of U.S. government

cabinet (KAB-in-it)—a group of advisers chosen by the president

candidate (KAN-di-date)—a person who runs for office

citizen (SIT-i-zuhn)—a person who is part of a nation by birth or choice

executive (eg-ZEK-yuh-tiv)—the branch of government that makes sure laws are followed

judicial (joo-DISH-uhl)—the branch of government that explains laws

legislative (lej-uh-SLAY-tiv)—the branch of government that passes bills that become laws

term (TURM)—a set period of time

Read More

Davis, Kenneth C. *The Presidents.* Don't Know Much About. New York: HarperCollins, 2002.

McNamara, Kevin J. *The Presidency.* Your Government—How It Works. Philadelphia: Chelsea House, 2000.

St. George, Judith. *So You Want To Be President?* New York: Philomel, 2000.

Internet Sites

Do you want to find out more about the U.S. Presidency? Let FactHound, our fact-finding hound dog, do the research for you.

Here's how:
1) Go to *http://www.facthound.com*
2) Type in the **Book ID** number: **0736822895**
3) Click on **FETCH IT**.

FactHound will fetch Internet sites picked by our editors just for you!

Index